BEAVERS

Edited by Kari A. Cornell

Printed in China

03   04   05   06   5   4   3   2

Library of Congress Cataloging-in-Publication Data

Rue, Leonard Lee.
Beavers / text and photographs by Leonard Lee Rue III.
p. cm. — (World life library)
Includes bibliographical references (p.70–71).
Summary: Presents information about the American beaver, including habitat,
physical characteristics, life cycle, behavior, and building skills.
ISBN 0–89658–548–4 (alk. paper)
1. Beavers—Juvenile literature. [1. American beaver. 2. Beavers.] I. Title. II. Series.

QL737.R632 R839 2001
599.37—dc21

Distributed in Canada by Raincoast Books, 9050 Shaughnessy Street, Vancouver, B.C. V6P 6E5

Published by Voyageur Press, Inc.
123 North Second Street, P.O. Box 338, Stillwater, MN 55082 U.S.A.
651-430-2210, fax 651-430-2211

Educators, fundraisers, premium and gift buyers, publicists, and marketing managers:
Looking for creative products and new sales ideas? Voyageur Press books are available at special discounts
when purchased in quantities, and special editions can be created to your specifications.
For details contact the marketing department at 800-888-9653.

Cover photograph by: Len Rue, Jr.
Back cover photograph by: Uschi Rue
Photograph on page 1: Uschi Rue
Photograph on page 4: Len Rue, Jr.
Photograph on page 6: Uschi Rue

BEAVERS

Text and photography by
Dr. Leonard Lee Rue III

**WORLDLIFE
LIBRARY**

Voyageur Press

Dedication

This book is dedicated to my lovely wife Ursula (Uschi) Rue and to her parents Maria & Josef Döhner. I am thankful to them for her.

Acknowledgments

No one can write a book of this scope based solely on his or her own experiences. My own personal experiences with beavers span more than fifty years. I have spent thousands of hours studying and photographing beavers. But even that is not enough. I have not been able to ear tag or radio collar beavers. Nor have I been able to conduct long captive observations, as I do not have access to laboratory facilities. I am thankful, though, to the researchers who have done such research and have documented their findings. I have combined their discoveries with my own observations in an attempt to give you an accurate, well-rounded account of beavers and how they live.

My thanks go to all of the researchers whose books are listed in my bibliography. They have all done an outstanding job and I have learned from each and every one of them. Lewis H. Morgan, whose book was first published in 1868, did an exceptionally outstanding job.

My thanks go to my close friends, Joe Taylor, Leon Kitchen, and all of the Spaces at Space Farms, who helped me with captive beavers. My special thanks go to Kari Cornell, my editor at Voyageur Press. Kari is a joy to work with. Thanks to my secretary, Marilyn Maring, for deciphering what I call writing and turning it into a printed page. And my thanks, as well, to my son, Len Rue, Jr. who has contributed many of the fine photos in this book. Each photo reminds us of the good times we have spent together all over North America. And last, but definitely not least, an extra special thanks to my lovely wife, Ursula (Uschi) Rue, who shares not only my life, but my love of beavers. Many of her photos have been included in this book. Some of our happiest moments were spent sitting quietly on a pond's edge watching beavers.

Contents

The Beaver

With the exception of man, no creature has been known to alter its environment as much as the beaver. Deer may overgraze, completely changing the composition of the vegetation found in forested areas. When elephants overpopulate and overfeed in an area, they can change brushland to desert. Many animals and some birds, such as geese, denude areas by overgrazing, causing extreme erosion. But only a beaver can transform a trickle of water into a pond or lake, eventually changing a forest to an open area.

Beavers thrive in deep, still waters. Underwater escape is the beaver's best defense against natural predators, such as humans and wolves. If the beaver cannot find a natural source of deep water, the animal will use sticks, brush, or anything else around to dam the water. Years later, when food sources such as aspen, willow, and alder saplings are depleted, the beaver leaves the pond or lake it has created. In time, the lake will again become a pond, which will become a swamp, which will become a marsh, which will become a meadow, which will perhaps again become a forested area with a trickle of water flowing through it.

General Characteristics

The beaver is a member of the rodent family, which, with its 2,052 species, is the largest order of mammals in the world. *Castor canadensis*, the North American beaver, and *Castor fiber*, the Eurasian beaver, were once widely distributed over North America, Europe, and Asia. There is no apparent difference between *canadensis* and *fiber* in size, weight, and shape. Where *canadensis* has been introduced into Europe, it readily breeds with *fiber*. Many biologists no longer consider the beaver to be two separate species. Often they classify all beaver as *Castor fiber*.

Casteroides, a prehistoric beaver, once swam in the freshwater lakes of North America. The beaver weighed up to 800 pounds (363 kg) and was as large as a big black bear. It measured 8 to 9 feet (244 cm to 274 cm) in length and had a 14-inch (36-cm) skull. In Europe, the prehistoric *Trogontherium,* was 20 percent larger than the modern beaver, which can grow to weigh as much as 110 pounds (50 kg).

A beaver out of the water is always on alert, ears pricked, nose turned to the wind, and eyes wide, watching for predators. (Leonard Lee Rue III)

The average adult beaver weighs between 40 and 60 pounds (18–27 kg) and measures between 48 inches and 54 inches (122–137 cm) in length. One-year-old beavers average 13 pounds (5.9 kg) while two-year-old beavers average 22 pounds (9.9 kg). The beaver averages between 8 and 9 inches (20–23 cm) in height at the shoulder.

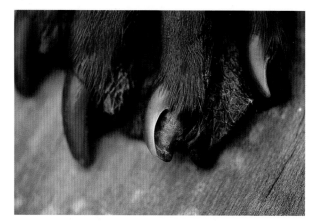

A beaver's hind feet are webbed to aid in swimming. The two inside toe nails on the beaver's hind foot are split and used to comb through tangled fur. (Leonard Lee Rue III)

Beavers have two layers of fur. Stiff, reddish, guard hairs, measuring about 2 inches (5 cm) in length, protect the undercoat from excessive wear. The soft, dense undercoat is ¾ inch (2 cm) thick and dark grayish-brown in color. This undercoat keeps the beaver warm. The guard hairs are either plucked or cut if the beaver's pelt is to be used for a fur coat. If you were to look at the hair of the undercoat under a microscope, you would see that each hair is made up of tiny scales, arranged in an overlapping pattern like shingles.

Historically, the beaver's luxurious coat has been its most valuable asset. During the early 1800s, beaver pelts were highly valued and trade in beaver fur reached its peak. The pelts were made into felt for beaver hats. When the hat makers soaked and pounded the fur, the scaled hairs interlocked, making a very durable felt. Beaver skins were used to make glue.

Beaver fur ranges from light tan to dark brown in color. Most beavers have dark brown fur with a reddish sheen. Northern beavers of both the North American and Eurasian breeds are darker in color than are southern beavers. Some of the northern beavers are almost jet-black. Albino beavers, although rare, do exist.

The beaver constantly grooms and oils its fur to keep it waterproof. To groom itself, a beaver sits upright with its tail bent between its back legs so it protrudes in front, exposing the cloaca—an orifice that contains the ducts for the beaver's genitals, alimentary system, urological system, oil glands, and castoreum glands. The beaver shakes the water out of its ears and uses its forepaws to scrub its ears and

When grooming, beavers use the combing claws on the hind foot to comb through their fur. (Leonard Lee Rue III)

face. Then it thoroughly scrubs its shoulders and rotund belly. Using the combing claws on its hind feet, the beaver combs its front shoulders, sides, and belly. The beaver then uses its forefeet to retrieve oil from its inverted oil glands and rubs it carefully all over its body. The creamy-yellow waterproofing oil is secreted by two small glands located near the cloaca's opening. Without waterproofing, the beaver would soon become water soaked and would be unable to tolerate the cold.

The beaver's Latin name, *castor,* comes from the two large castoreum glands that, in a large beaver, are 5 inches (13 cm) in circumference. The castoreum produced in these glands is a thick, oily secretion that varies in color from a light to a dark yellow. Its main purpose is to mark the beaver's territory. It has a pungent, sweet smell that other mammals find attractive. In fact, castoreum is widely used as a base for perfume. Human body heat breaks down the oil and gradually releases the fragrances that have been mixed with it.

Perhaps the most distinctive feature of the beaver is its large, flat, oval-shaped tail. I have a dried beaver tail in front of me from a 45-pound (21-kg) beaver. The tail is covered with black scales and shaped like the sole of a shoe. It measures 11½ inches (29 cm) in length, and 5¼ inches (13 cm) at its widest point, and 2¾ inches (7 cm) where it joined the body. The tail measures a little more than 1 inch (2.3 cm) at its thickest point. The beaver uses its tail as a brace while sitting erect and as a rudder while swimming. The tail also gives the beaver added propulsion when it swims and allows the beaver to stabilize itself when it floats on top of the water. The beaver slaps its tail against the water to warn other beavers of danger.

All beavers have four large incisor teeth in the front of their mouths that continue to grow throughout the animal's life. The front surface of the teeth is coated with a bright, orange-brown, extremely tough enamel. Both the color and the strength of the enamel is caused by the iron in the animal's diet. Just as humans must clip their fingernails, all rodents must chew on hard substances to keep the enamel portion of their teeth from growing too long. The backside of the incisor teeth is composed of a softer dentine that wears away faster than the enamel. When beavers grind their top and bottom incisors against one another, their teeth take on a chisel shape. A fur flap covers the space between the front chewing teeth and the back molars to prevent water or wood chips from entering the beaver's mouth when the beaver cuts wood underwater. All told, the beaver has twenty teeth: four incisors and sixteen molars. Each of the flat-topped molars has eight folded enamel transverse ridges to facilitate the grinding of vegetation, no matter how coarse.

The beaver has five toes on both of its forefeet; each toe is equipped with a long, stout nail of varying lengths. The center nail measures ⅝ inch (1.6 cm) long. Although the beaver lacks an opposable thumb, the animal's forefeet are very facile and capable of digging and holding all sorts of food items, sticks, and stones. When swimming, beavers ball up their forefeet into little fists and hold them against their chest. Because the beaver does not use its forefeet in swimming, there is only a slight webbing between the second and third toes. Beavers have five toes on each of their hind feet, all joined with a web of black, leathery skin. The foot on an adult beaver measures 7 inches (18 cm) long and, when the toes are spread for swimming, the feet measure 6½ inches (17 cm) wide. The nails on the hind feet are larger, heavier, and straighter than those on the front feet.

A beaver uses its flat, paddle-shaped tail to balance, steer, and, when danger is present, to warn other beavers by slapping it on the water. (Leonard Lee Rue III)

The center toe nail is ¾ inch (1.9 cm) long. Each of the two inside toes on the back feet have slightly serrated double nails that the beaver uses for grooming. The second toe is more highly developed than the first.

Built to Swim

The beaver's body is designed for life in the water; its eyes, nose, and ears are located near the top of its flat skull, allowing the beaver to lie deep in the water, hidden from predators while still watching, smelling,

A beaver often uses its tail as a stabilizer to keep its body upright when floating on top of the water. (Uschi Rue)

and listening for danger. When swimming underwater, the beaver closes its valvular nose and ears to prevent water from seeping into them. Their eyes have nictitating membranes that slide over the eyeballs like underwater goggles, allowing the beaver to see while it swims.

A swimming beaver uses different strokes for different purposes. To swim leisurely along the surface, the beaver usually moves both of its hind feet in unison, gliding frequently with both feet extended behind to reduce friction. The beaver uses its front feet to turn aside the branches it may encounter while swimming underwater. When there are no obstacles underwater, beavers ball their front feet into little fists and carry them against the chest.

The beaver uses its tail as a rudder to help it turn corners. When the beaver tows branches, it twists its tail to offset the drag of the branches, which ordinarily would cause it to swim in a circle. When swimming underwater, the beaver moves its tail up and down to propel it forward. When the beaver feeds on branches or removes the bark from a stick while floating on the surface, it will raise its tail slightly above the water's surface, touching just the tip of the tail to the water for balance.

To swim with speed, the beaver strokes with the left hind foot and then the right, alternately. No matter which method the beaver uses, it folds the toes of its hind foot together and curls its toes slightly to reduce drag. The beaver's webbed back feet enable it to swim more efficiently.

The beaver has other special features that allow it to swim underwater and remain submerged for long periods of time. The beaver's heartbeat slows down. This reduces the flow of blood to the beaver's extremities, conserving oxygen for the brain. The beaver's large lungs allow it to hold more air. Its oversized liver has greater capacity to store oxygenated blood. The beaver is also capable of exchanging at least 75 percent of its lung capacity when it surfaces. Humans, on the other hand, can only exchange 15 to 20 percent.

Under ordinary conditions, a beaver remains submerged for about 3 to 5 minutes. But Edward R. Warren and several other researchers have observed beavers staying under water for as long as 15 minutes. Researchers generally agree that a beaver can swim submerged for distances of ½ mile (0.8 km) or more.

Sensing and Communicating

Like humans, beavers have five senses. The beaver's most highly developed sense is smell, the sense upon which the beaver is most dependent. I can find no record of scientists testing the beaver's sense of smell, but I think it would be safe to say that their sense of smell is equal to that of a deer, which has been proven to be hundreds of times more sensitive than a human's.

Beavers are, for the most part, nocturnal animals. When it is time for the beaver to begin their evening activities, the yearlings or the adults will emerge from the lodge, swim 20 to 50 feet (6.1–15 m), void their bodily waste, and return to the lodge. The male usually swims slowly about, checking the perimeter of the pond for damage. His nose, raised in the air, twitches in short sniffs. When satisfied that no danger lurks nearby, the beaver will begin to feed on the downwind side of the pond. This will insure that he will detect the scent of any creature that moves on the upwind side of the pond.

The beaver's sense of hearing is exceptionally keen. Although the animal's head and ears are small, the beaver's auditory canal is as large as a human's. Because beavers feed mainly on twigs, bark, and soft vegetation, they are noisy eaters. They pause often while feeding to listen for danger.

The beaver's small eyes lead many to believe that the animal has poor eyesight. I have no idea of just what beavers see. I do know that beavers have extremely detailed mental maps of their surroundings. I have spent hundreds and hundreds of hours researching the beavers that live on Horseshoe Lake in Denali National Park, Alaska. Once, I was sitting in a patch of dwarf birch and willow across the pond from where a group of beavers were cutting aspen saplings. I had draped a piece of camouflage netting over me and my camera. The first beaver to swim around the point of land on which the lodge was located changed its direction and swam straight towards me, slapping its tail in warning. The wind was blowing toward me so I knew the beaver could not smell me. The beaver could not recognize me as a man because I looked like a rounded mound rising 3 feet (0.9 m) above the brush. I was, however, a mound that had not been there the day before, and the beaver was able to recognize that. At a distance of about 450 feet (137 m), the beaver "saw" me. Similar incidences happened many times.

The beaver's sense of taste is well developed, as can be seen in its preference for certain foods and avoidance of others. The beaver uses its whiskers, eyebrows, tail, and the soles of its feet—all well endowed with sensory nerve endings—to touch.

The beaver has four rows of whiskers, or vibrissae, that are 3 to 4 inches (7.6–10 cm) long. Like a cat's whiskers, they are sensory devices that tell the beaver if its body will fit through an opening. If a beaver can enter a tunnel without having its whiskers touch the side, the beaver's body will fit through the opening. The vibrissae also help the beaver to avoid underwater obstacles.

Adult beavers communicate through sound; they hiss when angry, emit a chur sound when they feel threatened, and let out a prolonged OOOOOOOOOH sound when they are content. Young beavers frequently whine petulantly. The most commonly used form of communication is the slap of the tail on water. The tail slap of an adult beaver is extremely loud and, if unexpected, can be both startling and unnerving. Many people believe that a beaver tail slap on the water will send all beavers within earshot diving to the depths of the pond. Not so. Although tail slaps always signal potential danger, the degree of danger varies.

Beavers slap their wide, flat tails on the water to warn other members of the colony that danger is near. (Len Rue, Jr.)

The tail slap of a baby beaver or of a yearling beaver is seldom taken seriously by others. The louder and more powerful tail slap of an adult beaver causes beavers to take immediate action. Those beavers on land will move into the water. Beavers in shallow water will move out to deep water while those in deep water will swim back and forth to try to catch the scent of the potential predator.

Beavers are much more likely to slap their tails in response to scent rather than in response to sight or sound. An alarmed beaver will raise its tail perpendicular to the surface of the water, dunk its head and shoulders into the water, and swing its tail down to strike the water. All of this happens in a second, and it's much too fast for the human eye to catch.

Eating and Digestion

The beaver's favorite foods are the twigs and bark from aspen, willow, and alder saplings. In the spring and summer, beavers will also eat skunk cabbage, grasses, and berries. Beavers have to eat a lot of these fibrous foods to get the nutrition they need. An adult beaver will need 1½ to 2 pounds (0.7–0.9kg) of food per day for body maintenance. In autumn, the beaver will eat as much as 3 pounds (1.4 kg) of food in an effort to build up fat reserves on its body. The layer of fat found under its skin provides the beaver with additional insulation. Extra fat is also stored in its tail.

This beaver uses its forefeet to bring leaves and twigs to its mouth. (Uschi Rue)

The beaver has a large stomach for food storage and processing. It has an even larger caecum at the beginning of its large intestines where the fibrous material is further digested. The beaver gains nutrition from the tree's outer and inner barks; it cannot break down the lignin in the wood itself.

Like most rodents, beavers are coprophagous. They eat so much bulk material that some of it passes from their bodies as green feces before being fully digested. Beavers eat the green feces, and, when passed through the body the second time, essential nutrients are absorbed and the feces emerge brown.

The beaver has four incisor teeth, two on the bottom and two on the top, that grow throughout the beaver's life. The iron in the beaver's diet causes the teeth to turn orange. (Leonard Lee Rue III)

Nature's Architect

An established beaver colony, one that has been occupied for two or more years, will have six or seven beavers living in one lodge. The colony usually consists of the adult male and female, two or three year-lings—young beavers that are more than a year old, and two or three kits—baby beavers. At age two, beavers look for a mate with which to raise a family. Together they search for a place to build a lodge. By the following spring, the lodge will be teeming with the energy of two or three kits. The kits will stay with the colony until they are two years old, helping to raise the next set of kits the following spring. The second spring, yearlings strike out on their own to look for a mate and build their own lodge.

When a beaver, or a pair of beavers, move into a new area, its first priority is shelter. If there is a streamside bank higher than 24 inches (67 cm), the beaver can dig a bank burrow. The beaver dives beneath the water's surface and, using the strong claws on its forefeet, digs an underwater tunnel into the bank. The beaver will dig the tunnel to slope upwards, above the water level, where it will excavate a small chamber. When digging a tunnel, the beaver will only use its forefeet at first. But as the tunnel lengthens, the beaver will loosen the dirt with its forefeet and then use its hind feet to kick the dirt out the entrance. The beaver must come to the surface every five to ten minutes to replenish its oxygen supply. When the beaver tunnels above the water level, enough air will usually filter through the porous earth to allow the beaver to breathe in the chamber it is excavating. At first, the chamber may be only 24 inches (61 cm) across by 18 inches (46 cm) high—just large enough to accommodate a pair of beavers sleeping side by side.

If the beavers cannot find a bank that is tall enough, they will take temporary shelter beneath a dense bush or exposed tree root—anything that will provide cover while they sleep. If they have not chosen a location on an existing pond or lake, the beavers must begin to construct a dam.

Beaver dams are a marvel of engineering—especially when you consider that they are built by a pair of two-year-old animals, each weighing an average of about 35 pounds (16 kg), working without tools,

Alaskan beavers built this dam with whatever brush they could find, including dwarf willow, birch, and alder. The lodge, visible to the right in the distance, is actually connected to the dam. (Leonard Lee Rue III)

and using whatever materials are at hand. Most of the time, beavers select good dam sites. I've often thought that moving some dams up or down the stream a short distance would make the beaver's work easier. But the beaver, once determined to build on a site, cannot be swayed. The beaver is one of nature's most persistent creatures. The farmers, road crews, railroad crews, and others who have had to repeat-edly remove beaver dams that flooded crops, timber, highways, and railroad culverts will agree.

A beaver tows three branches, butt-end first, to the dam site. (Uschi Rue)

On two occasions, I have watched beavers build dams from beginning to end. The first was on the small stream flowing out of Horseshoe Lake in Denali National Park. The stream was about 8 feet (2.4 m) wide and perhaps 18 inches (46 cm) deep, and the dam was the sixth in a series of seven. The beavers seemed to have picked this particular spot because the water tumbled over some stones, cre-ating a riffle. Beavers are often stimulated to build a dam in response to the sound of tumbling water. The second dam was on a small, quiet stream flowing from Coffin Lac in the Canadian province of Quebec. This is a very flat region and the dam backed up the water for almost a half mile (0.8 km).

No beaver dam looks exactly like another. Beavers tailor the dams to fit the space in which they're built. The highest dam I have seen was in a narrow gorge on a little stream near Centennial, Wyoming. From the water level on the downstream side, it measured 14 feet (4.3 m) high. I saw one of the longest dams built entirely of sticks near Homer, New York. This 800-foot (244–m) dam wandered all over a marsh and did not seem to serve any real purpose as the water below it was almost as deep as the water above it. At Space Farms in Beemerville, New Jersey, I saw a dam that was at least 1,320 feet (402 m)

A beaver carries a branch into its lodge via the underwater tunnel. (Leonard Lee Rue III)

long. In the construction of this dam, the beavers had used sticks, stones, and mud to build the center of the dam right where the stream's current flowed through the marsh. Along the shore, where there was no current, the beavers used only mud and grass to block the water. I have noticed that beavers often pile up mud and grass where there is minimal water pressure.

Beavers use their forefeet to place rocks on the dam. The rocks help compress the branches and twigs, holding them in place. (Uschi Rue)

If there are not sticks available, beavers will build dams out of whatever they can find. The oddest dam I have seen was constructed entirely out of cornstalks. In the 1960s, Van Campen's brook near Blairstown, New Jersey had banks 8 feet (2.4 m) high. There was very little brush growing along the banks, but hundreds of acres of cornfields on both sides. The beavers lived in a burrow in the bank, ate the corn, and used the stalks for their dam.

In their studies of beaver in Wyoming, James Grasse and Eriven Putnam photographed a dam that was only 30 feet (9.1 m) wide, but 18 feet (5.5 m) high. The longest dam that I can find on record was built more than 100 years ago near the town of Berlin, New Hampshire. It was more than 4,000 feet (1,219 m) long and created a lake that housed forty beaver lodges. In the Voronzeh reserve, located halfway between Moscow and the Black Sea, there is a dam near the town of Marinka that is 393 feet (120 m) long by 3 feet 2 inches (1 m) wide.

When a beaver plans to fell a tree, it carefully checks the air for the scent of any predator. If all is safe, the beaver leaves the water and selects the tree to be felled. Rising up on its hind feet and holding its front feet against the tree, the beaver sniffs the bark and then turns its head sideways to make the first bite. The beaver holds the teeth in its upper jaw solidly against the bark and opens the lower jaw wide to make the cut. The beaver's lower teeth, powered by its massive masseter muscles, are forced through the bark and wood, making a 45-degree cut. After making the first bite, which is usually the top cut, the beaver moves its jaws down the tree, and, holding its head upside-down, makes the lower cut. This cut also measures 45 degrees. Together, the two cuts measure 90 degrees, the most efficient angle and one humans strive for when chopping down a tree with an ax. The length of the chip the beaver cuts out of the tree is about equal to the diameter of the tree. The beaver cuts the chip at both ends and tears it loose from the tree. The beaver may cut all around the tree or, if the tree is on a slope, the beaver may do all the cutting on the uphill side. As the beaver cuts toward the center of the tree, each succeeding chip is smaller than the last .

Using its incisor teeth, the beaver pulls a bulky log over the top of the dam to the side that faces downstream. The weight of the log will help compress the dam and give it strength. (Uschi Rue)

As the tree starts to lean, the remaining wood fibers creak as they tear apart. The beaver dashes to the water to escape from the falling tree and to hide from any predator that may appear to investigate the crack and splash sounds made by the falling tree. Occasionally beavers miscalculate and are killed by the tree they were felling. I once watched a beaver dash under a sapling as it was falling. If that sapling had been a full-grown tree, it probably would have killed the beaver.

After the tree has come crashing down, the beaver floats on the water some distance away, watching to make sure there is no danger. Then the beaver and other members of the colony feed on the leaves.

To build a dam, beavers swim upstream from the chosen dam site to cut brush. Grasping the butt end of the brush in its teeth, the beaver pulls, tows, and floats the brush to the dam site. If the stream bottom is soft, the beaver will use its teeth and forepaws to jab the brush into the earth. If the stream bottom is rocky, the beaver will push the brush into the river bank. The beaver weaves succeeding pieces

Balancing its weight on its hind feet, the beaver carries a load of twigs and mud between its forefeet and mouth. (Uschi Rue)

of brush with the first until a layer of brush spans the stream along the bottom. Beavers incorporate any protruding rocks in the stream bed into the dam's base. Beavers next place stones and mud on top of the brush to weigh it down and compress it. At this stage, the water that flows through the brush usually does not wash it away. Once the first layer is anchored, the beaver uses its teeth to push and pin sticks as thick as 1 inch (2.5 cm) in diameter into the mass of brush. When it has pushed the sticks as far into the dam as possible, the beaver then chews the sticks off to make them flush with the top of the dam. The beaver places all of the brush, poles, and small logs with the butt end downstream, just as they carried them to the dam. Beavers never turn a branch to place it on the dam.

After the beaver has built a secure base for the dam that rises above the water level, it will begin to use mud to fill holes in the dam. The beaver will get most of the mud from the area in front of the water face of the dam, making the water deeper there than in the rest of the pond. Diving down, the beaver digs up a large load of mud, carrying it beneath its chin and between its forefeet. The beaver uses its forefeet to push the mud in between the pieces of brush that make up the face of the dam. At first, the force of the water flowing through the brush pushes the mud through, but gradually the mud clogs the dam. Beavers apply mud to the dam until the brush is a solid mass and the face is entirely covered. The mud prevents the water from passing through the dam, causing the water level to rise.

The beaver uses the water surface as a natural level, to make sure that it is building the dam uniformly. As the water level rises, beavers add new material to the top and the sides of the dam to keep everything even. Using its teeth, the beaver pulls and pushes larger sticks, poles, and logs over the top of the dam, sliding them down the face to reinforce the dam on the downstream side. New dams are narrow at the apex—so narrow that a person walking on the dam will compress it below the water level. As the beaver continues to add new material to the dam, it becomes thicker and sturdier, allowing big animals such as bears and moose to use the dam as a bridge.

The dam is basically a scalene triangle, with each side varying in length. The beaver constructs the dam so that the angle of each face of the dam has a different degree of steepness. I have found that the downstream side is usually between 30 and 40 degrees. The upstream face of the dam is often 1½ times longer than is the downstream face, as this greatly strengthens the dam.

A beaver dam does not hold back the water that flows into the pond it created. Most of the water, except what is lost to evaporation, seeps either through the dam or around the edges to continue flowing downstream. When the dam secures the necessary water depth, the beavers build a lodge. Beavers build different kinds of lodges based on the conditions at the site. If they have already built a

A beaver packs mud into the dam's upstream face. This eventually seals the dam, backing up the water on the upstream side. (Uschi Rue)

burrow into the bank, beavers may pile a mound of brush and mud on top of the underground chamber. This reinforces the shelter and helps to prevent predators from digging down through the earth to get to the sleeping chamber. When they build the mound 4 feet to 6 feet (1.2–1.8 m) high, beavers may cut a new chamber into the mound of piled up materials. Or the beaver may leave the bank burrow as it is; most colonies have three or four bank burrows that can be used in emergencies.

When a pond's banks are low, beavers build an island-type lodge. The beavers find an area where the water is about 4 feet (1.2 m) deep. In northern climates, the water has to be at least 4 feet (1.2 m) deep to leave a space beneath the ice that may freeze to a depth of 2 feet (0.6 m) or more. Starting at the bottom of the pond, beavers pile brush, sticks, logs, mud, and stones in a mass until the structure is raised above the water level to a height of 6 feet (1.8 m) or more. As they do when they build dams, beavers dig up mud from around the base of the lodge and use it to seal the lodge. This also increases the water depth around the lodge. When they've built the lodge at least 4 feet (1.2 m) above the surface of the water, the beavers dive underwater and begin to chew and cut a tunnel into the center of the structure. They also hollow out an above-water living chamber. They do not, as people once believed, leave a hollow center while piling up the material that will form the living chamber. Beavers continue to make changes to the living chamber as long as they live in the lodge. When the beavers have cut all of the saplings along the water's edge, for example, they raise the dam to extend the pond farther back into the woods they are cutting. With the rise in water level, beavers must cut the roof of the chamber higher and raise the floor to keep the living area dry. New material is also added to the outside of the lodge so, although the chamber is enlarged, the walls maintain their thickness.

I have had the opportunity to cut two island beaver lodges in half and examine their construction. In both instances, the beavers had been removed and transplanted because their dams were constantly flooding out roads.

The outside dimensions of one lodge were 11 feet (3.4 m) across at the water level and 5 feet (1.5 m) high. The inverted, bowl-like living chamber was approximately 4 feet 6 inches (1.4 m) across by 2 feet (0.6 m) high. Three underwater tunnels, each measuring about 16 inches (41 cm) in diameter, led to the outside of the lodge. The outside entrances to these tunnels were about 2 feet (0.6 m) below the water's surface.

A beaver tows branches over the top of the dam. Branches like these, with plenty of green leaves and tender shoots, are stored for food in the winter. (Uschi Rue)

Inside the lodge were several levels. The basic floor to the living chamber was 4 inches (10 cm) above the water level. This is where the beavers would sit to eat and to allow their fur to drip dry. The bed area, raised 10 inches (25 cm) above the water level, was covered with long, thin strips of wood, which looked just like excelsior. The beavers split the strips from saplings. Grasses are seldom used for bedding because they would rot.

To facilitate traveling in the shallower parts of the pond, beavers dig channels in the pond bottom. These channels are usually 18 inches to 24 inches (46–61 cm) wide and just as deep. Even in times of severe drought, when the pond level drops, these channels allow beavers to travel in comparative safety.

Beavers seldom construct just one dam, although the construction of that first dam is imperative.

As time allows, beavers usually construct additional auxiliary dams, usually upstream and downstream from their main dam. An auxiliary dam below the main dam will back up water against the base of the main dam, reducing upstream pressure on it. Upstream dams put more food in close proximity to water as the water floods back into the timber. Because beavers are most vulnerable when they are on land, having water close to the trees they are cutting is a tremendous safety feature. Upstream dams make it easier for beavers to transport food to the main lodge.

The entrance to this beaver lodge is usually underwater, but weeks of dry weather have left it exposed. Submerged entrances are yet another defense against predators, most of which can't swim underwater. (Uschi Rue)

If the land surrounding a beaver lodge is fairly level and beavers have harvested all of the food that is close to the water, they often dig canals to reach trees that are farther back. Beavers usually dig the earth loose, cut off roots, remove rocks, and pile the debris on either side of the canal. I have seen canals with only 8 inches to 12 inches (20–30 cm) of water in the bottom, but the beavers usually try to have at least 18 inches (46 cm) of water so that they can swim and float the logs they are towing. They also dig the canals as straight as possible to make it easier to haul the saplings back to the main pond. The longest canal on record was discovered by Enos Mills in the Lily Lakes colony near Long's Peak, Colorado. It was 750 feet (228 m) long and 3 feet (0.9 m) deep.

When they've exhausted food sources along the pond's edge, beavers dig canals to reach trees that are farther away. This canal measures 70 feet (21 m) long. (Len Rue, Jr.)

Spring

March 21 is the spring equinox, when the sun is positioned directly over the equator. For most of North America, Europe, and Asia, there are exactly twelve hours of daylight and twelve hours of darkness on this first day of spring. A designated day on the calendar, however, often has little to do with the reality of the weather. March is a most treacherous month, often promising much more than it delivers. But each year is different. In 2000, the northeastern United States experienced one of the wettest summers on record. A year before the same area suffered severe drought.

The arrival of spring also depends upon where you live on the globe. Spring usually advances north at the rate of 15 miles (24 km) per day. The season works its way up mountainsides at the rate of 100 vertical feet (30 m) per day. Knowing this, it makes sense that the beaver activity I have observed on a given spring day along the Rio Grande River in Big Bend National Park, Texas, differs from the activity I would observe on the same day just south of the Brooks Mountain Range in Alaska. Naturally spring comes to the beaver colonies in both of those places at different times.

Beavers in most of the southern part of North America and Eurasia don't experience a real winter. Some areas may get freezing nights with ice on the ponds, and they definitely get winter at the higher elevations, but for practical purposes, there is no real winter south of the thirty-ninth parallel. The examples in the following chapters are of beavers living north of that parallel.

The ice usually melts out of the ponds in the northern United States during the first part of March and in Alaska in the middle to the end of May. Because of the Gulf Stream, Northern Europe's spring weather is about two weeks earlier than the weather in North America on the same parallel.

Although most of the beaver ponds have remained ice covered, there are usually spots in many ponds that open earlier or have remained ice free throughout the winter. Ponds that are spring fed never freeze entirely. The 56°F (14°C) spring water that bubbles into the pond from below the frost line—where the Earth's temperature remains constant—will keep a hole open. Beavers seek out such spots to

Beavers welcome the taste of the yellow pond lily's tender flowers, leaves, and roots after a long winter of eating primarily bark. (Leonard Lee Rue III)

look for food above the ice. Skunk cabbage, with an internal heat of 76°F (25°C), pushes up through the ice and snow in January and is the first fresh food of the season for beavers. As the temperature of the air rises to 35°F (2°C), the frost melts from the ground and green grasses begin to sprout. At 44°F (7°C), the buds on the aspen, willow, and alder begin to swell. If the warm weather continues, the buds soon burst open, producing green foliage. For the beaver, restricted to a diet of bark from the food supply they stored last autumn, this change to a fresh diet is most welcome. The rhizomes, leaves, and flowers of both the yellow and white pond lilies are favorite foods. Beavers eat grasses, sedges, ferns, many types of forbs, flags, fungi, berries, mushrooms, duckweed, and, as the water warms, algae.

When skunk cabbage bursts forth from the marsh floor in the early spring, beavers feast on the plant's crunchy green leaves and blossoms. (Leonard Lee Rue III)

Beavers do very little work on their dams or lodges in the spring. They check the dam each evening, but only make routine maintenance repairs. They fix any damage that may have occurred over the winter. Heightening or extending the dam will have to wait until later in the year.

It is in the spring that beavers give birth to kits. The gestation period for the beaver is 105 to 107 days, with most beaver kits being born in April, May, or very early June. The beaver's average litter size is four kits. Beavers giving birth for the first time may have just two or three kits. The male beaver usually leaves the lodge several days before the female gives birth, taking up temporary residence in a burrow lodge. He returns to the lodge after the female has had the kits.

The female gives birth in the lodge, sitting in the same position she uses to get oil from her cloaca when grooming—upright with her tail bent under and forward so that she can easily reach her cloaca. She does not assist in the birth but immediately picks up the newborn kit and removes the placenta with her teeth. She uses her tongue to wash the blood from the kit's fur. Subsequent kits may be born one to two hours apart. After the last kit is born, the mother promptly eats the discharged afterbirth to restore the nutrients expended in the birthing process.

At birth, a baby beaver weighs 1 pound (0.5 kg) and measures 12 inches (30 cm) long. Singletons (the name for the kit when its the only one in the litter) have weighed as much as 1½ pounds (0.7 g) and measured 16 inches (40 cm) long. The kits are born fully furred with their eyes and ears open and their incisor teeth bursting through their gums. The incisors are white at first and then gradually change to orange. The kits are born knowing how to swim, but are not yet able to dive down through the tunnel to get out of the lodge.

The mother beaver will carry her kits in her mouth when she wants to get them back into the lodge. (Leonard Lee Rue III)

Under normal conditions, the kits come out of the lodge for the first time at about three weeks of age. Once, while I was observing beavers at Denali's Horseshoe Lake, the lodge tunnels were exposed due to a drought. A beaver kit swam out of the lodge and across the lake toward where I was standing. A few moments later the mother beaver appeared and, upon seeing the little one, paddled over, took the kit crossways in her mouth, and swam back across the lake and into the lodge. When kits make their first outings, they are usually accompanied by the adult beavers. Kits swim alongside of the adults, hold on to the adults' fur, and sometimes ride on the adults' backs or tails. As the kits become older, the adults discourage clinging by simply diving underwater to force the young to swim on their own.

Beaver kits nurse until they are at least two months old and then they are weaned. Females nurse their young in the privacy and safety of the lodge. When the kits are about three days old, they begin to eat various green vegetation that the adults carry into the lodge. Yearling beavers help feed the babies, too. Like yearling wolves in a pack, yearling beavers are very solicitous of the young, grooming them, carrying food to them, and playing with them.

Beaver kits are very vocal. The kits, used to the constant attention of the yearlings and the adults, act like spoiled children. Their almost constant whining for more food and attention can be heard through the walls of the lodge.

As the mother eats, her seven-day-old kit swims close by. (Leonard Lee Rue III)

The kits don't gather food for themselves, but hasten to feed upon any food that the yearlings or the adults bring into the lodge. By the time the kits are two months old, they can debark a twig as neatly as an adult. They may sit upright along the edge of the shore or float on the surface of the water as they feed. Beavers eat the bark from twigs much as a person eats corn from a cob. The beavers hold the twig in their fore-paws, and starting from one end, they remove about 1 inch (2.5 cm) of the bark, then roll the twig slightly and remove another strip. They continue stripping and rolling until they have removed every vestige of bark and then discard the twig.

In April, when the yearlings reach the age of twenty-two months, most of them respond to an innate urge to move out of the parental colony, seek a mate, and start a colony of their own. Adult beavers encourage the yearling beavers to leave the colony to prevent inbreeding and the premature depletion of the food supply.

When they disperse, most beavers go downstream to look for unoccupied territory. Beavers (especially the males) are very territorial. One of the first things that the adult beavers do after the ice melts is mark the perimeter of their territory with castoreum. The beavers make "castor paddies" or "scent mounds" to advertise their presence and ownership. They gather up an armful of mud and debris from

Top: Two kits less than six weeks old nibble on birch leaves. They are also able to remove bark from saplings on their own. (Len Rue, Jr.)

Bottom: Three six-week-old beaver kits huddle together for safety. (Len Rue, Jr.)

the pond bottom, hold it beneath their chin, and carry it to a spot about 2 feet (0.6 m) from the water's edge where they make a mound. Beavers use some of these mounds repeatedly. I have seen some mounds that were as high as 2 feet (0.6 m). To deposit castoreum, beavers straddle the mound, evert their castoreum glands, and drag them across the mound.

An adult beaver marks the colony's territory by dragging castoreum across a castor paddy. The castor's scent tells other beavers that the pond is already occupied. (Len Rue, Jr.)

Other beavers pick up the scent of castoreum from quite a distance. When castoreum, being an oil, is washed into the water by rain or deposited there directly by the beaver, it carries information, such as the beaver's age and sex, downstream for many miles. When traveling through an area already occupied by a colony, two-year-old beavers searching for a place to call home do not ordinarily scent mark. As long as the transient beavers do not stop, the resident beavers will leave them alone. If a stray male should deposit some of his own scent on a resident's scent mound, or stop to feed, the angry resident male would drive him off by hissing loudly. If the bluff didn't work, the resident beaver would attack. More than likely the bluff would work. The adult resident's much larger size would be enough to scare away the younger male. Beavers seldom fight.

Unless a female beaver is nursing, as this one is, it's difficult to tell a male from a female by sight. This female's nipples are clearly visible when she stands on her hind feet. (Uschi Rue)

Summer

It is high praise when we say of a person that he or she is as "busy as a beaver," or that he or she "works like a beaver." And it is true that, at times, the beaver is very industrious. But in the summertime, the living is easy for beavers.

In most of the beaver's habitat, fresh vegetation grows in abundance through August. Beavers cut very few saplings and no trees during this time. Instead, they feed on the tender sprouts of aspen, willow, and birch. They carry mouthfuls of grass and sedge back to their lodges to eat. Berries of many kinds ripen and beavers eat them all, including the leaves and canes. In some areas, the surface of the beaver ponds are blanketed with the leaves of yellow and white water lilies. Beavers not only eat the flowers, but roll the large leaves inward from both sides to make them easier to eat. Mushrooms flourish from June through September, and beavers love them.

When foraging for food, especially with kits in tow, beavers have to be particularly watchful for predators. Summer is the time of year when predators are most active. Bobcats, lynxes, cougars, otters, wolves, black bears, and grizzly bears readily prey on beavers when the opportunity presents itself. The beaver's underwater tunnels and the deep water it has created around the lodge are its main protection against predators. The beaver is always on alert, listening and watching for danger as it feeds near the water's edge.

The kits spend a lot of their time playing with each other and with the yearlings. They swim and dive in unison like small porpoises. They stand upright in shallow water and "dance" by turning their bodies from side to side while raising their heads. They sometimes turn so far to the side and raise their heads so high that they fall over backward. The "dance" is often an invitation to another kit or yearling to play-wrestle. In play-wrestling, beavers clasp their forearms around each other's shoulders while holding their

Fireweed frames this view of a beaver dam and colony on Denali's Horsehoe Lake. (Leonard Lee Rue III)

Top: The tall, green grasses that edge many ponds and streams are a big part of the beaver's diet during the summer months. (Leonard Lee Rue III)
Bottom: Two kits splash and tumble in a play-wrestling match. (Uschi Rue)

heads cheek to cheek. In this upright position, the kits look like tiny sumo wrestlers as they try to push their opponents off balance. Although beavers may wrestle while standing in shallow water, they usually play in deeper water, kicking like mad with their hind feet to keep their heads above water. Such matches usually last for just a few minutes.

All is not play for the kits as they learn to "become little beaver." For the first couple of weeks, the kits are groomed extensively by their mother, but they soon learn to groom and oil their own coats. This is a most important lesson because all beavers spend considerable time each day grooming themselves. An unkempt beaver is a sick beaver.

The kits also learn by imitation the many duties required of all beavers. I once watched an adult beaver coat its lodge. While the adult was carrying large armloads of mud and debris in the bipedal posture, a two-month-old kit, walking on all fours, was carrying 4-inch sticks, which it placed on the top of the lodge.

In the summer, a beaver pond is not only a nursery for baby beavers, it is a mecca for many types of wildlife. Myriad types of insects lay their eggs in the water of the ponds, and the larvae provide food for the fish that live there. As the insects hatch and become airborne, birds also feed on them. Woodpeckers drill nest cavities into the trees killed by flooding and feed upon the insects and grubs that infest the dead trees.

The wolf, one of the beaver's many predators, hopes to catch beavers off-guard along the water's edge. (Len Rue, Jr.)

The assured supply of water and vegetation in beaver ponds provide ideal nesting spots for many types of ducks. The ducks feed on the vegetation and the insects. Hawks, owls, and eagles visit the pond to hunt the ducks and baby beaver for food. Moose and deer come to the ponds to drink, feed, and cool off.

By summer's end, the beaver family begins to think about where it will spend the winter months. Occasionally, a beaver family will have an additional lodge on a different pond and move back and forth between the lodges, probably to lessen exposure to parasites that tend to build up in any bird or animal home that's used for extended periods of time. If beavers move from one lodge to the other, they usually do so in late summer. The lodge they repair in late summer or early fall is the one in which they will spend the winter.

Beaver feed heavily upon willow, aspen, and birch sprouts during the summer. They cut the sprouts inland and then bring them to the water's edge to feed. (Len Rue, Jr.)

A yearling and a kit nibble the bark from an aspen log. (Len Rue, Jr.)

Autumn

In September, the days shorten and the shadows lengthen. Bright yellow goldenrod and scarlet red maples stand boldly against the autumn sky, and a nip in the night air displaces the heat and lethargy of August. By this time the shorebirds have migrated south, the squirrels are busy storing nuts, and the elk and European red deer enter the rutting season, the beaver begins its most active time of the year—preparing for winter.

The beaver's activities follow a logical sequence. At this time the beavers will have already built or selected the lodge in which they will spend the winter. They set to work lengthening, strengthening, and repairing their dam. If the water level is high, the beaver will raise the floor of the lodge and the roof of the sleeping chamber.

To strengthen the entire structure, the beaver adds new material to the roof of the lodge. The beaver pulls long sticks, stripped of their bark, vertically up to the apex of the lodge. Then the beaver shoves shorter sticks into the mass to pin it all together, cutting off the sticks that protrude from the surface of the lodge. When the exterior mass has a thickness of 2 feet (0.6 m) or more, the beaver coats the lodge with mud and fine debris.

Beavers usually have three to five pathways they follow to get out of the water and up to the roof of the lodge. When repairing the lodge, they work outward from these pathways. Beavers dredge up most of the material used to coat the lodge from all around the lodge base, greatly increasing the area's water depth. The beavers transform last winter's food sticks, which were fed upon, peeled, and discarded just outside the lodge's tunnels, into building material. Removing the debris is like cleaning out the cupboard—it makes space for the storage of the coming winter's food supply.

To coat the lodge, the beaver dives down to the bottom of the pond and gathers all of the mud and sticks it can possibly carry beneath its chin. Walking on its two hind legs and using its tail as a brace, the beaver staggers up the lodge as far as it can go. It often stumbles and drops the load along the way.

This pond is home to two beaver lodges. A beaver family may live part of the time in one lodge and part of the time in the other. The second lodge could also belong to the family yearlings after they move out of the main lodge. (Len Rue, Jr.)

This beaver is cutting a felled sapling in half before towing it to the lodge. (Uschi Rue)

No matter, the beaver just uses its front feet to smooth the pile into the surface of the lodge. Then it's back down for another load. Although the beavers may work on coating the lodge all night, after about six trips they stop to feed or to cut some food for winter. The apex of the lodge, with an average diameter of about 15 inches (38 cm), is not coated, allowing fresh air to filter down into the roof of the sleeping chamber. Just as people can see their own breath when exhaling on a winter's day, wisps of warm, moist air from the beavers' breath drift from the apex of the lodge. The cold turns the lodge's mud coating to the consistency of concrete, thwarting the predators' attempts to dig into the lodge. When the beaver pond freezes, predators are able to walk out to the lodge.

Notice how the beaver has to turn its head sideways to cut the chips from the sapling it is felling. (Len Rue, Jr.)

Once the lodge is in order, the beaver spends weeks gathering and storing food for the winter. Beavers place the winter food cache as close to the entrance of the lodge as possible. In fact, the cache often looks like an extension of the lodge itself. Most caches will contain two or more tons of saplings and branches. The beavers fell saplings and tow them to the lodge where they will be stored for winter food. If the branches are small, the beaver will often take three or four in its mouth at one time. Sometimes the logs to be towed are so big that the beaver can't get its mouth around them. The beaver then has to bite into the wood and hold it with its teeth to move it downstream. Many times, when an adult is swimming back with a sapling for the winter food pile, the beaver kits will hang on to the branches, feeding on the leaves as they are towed along. Sometimes they will simply chop off an entire branch and swim to shore to feed upon it. When the adult beaver reaches the lodge, it dives down and jabs the butt end of the branches into the mud at the bottom of the pond. When the first layer has been firmly anchored, succeeding layers will be woven into the preceding layers.

I have, on numerous occasions, seen yearling beaver pull in sections of logs that were too buoyant to anchor. The logs kept bobbing back up to the surface despite the splashing efforts of the yearling. Eventually, an adult would return with a load of its own and, upon seeing the problem, would retrieve the buoyant log and firmly anchor it in place.

A beaver tows a food branch to store in the winter food pile. (Len Rue, Jr.)

As more and more material is added to the winter food pile, many of the leaves and branches will stick out above the surface of the water. Kits and yearlings often eat these twigs. Their feeding does not diminish the amount of food available for winter as everything that sticks above the surface of the water will be lost to the beaver when the pond freezes over.

Yearling beavers do their part to help gather food, too. Even the kits add a few twigs to the pile on occasion. I once watched a yearling beaver haul a small twig for a distance of at least ¼ mile (0.4 km). The nutrition the yearling would obtain from the bark would not provide as much energy as the beaver used to bring that particular twig back to the lodge.

To survive the winter, a beaver colony will need to store between 1,500 and 2,500 pounds (681–1,135 kg) of edible bark, twigs, and leaves. Because they don't eat the wood, they must gather many tons of logs, saplings, and branches to get enough food to survive. Beavers appear to know when they have enough food stored to last them through the winter. They stop gathering at that time.

Southern beavers do not need to store food as their ponds seldom freeze over. However, like northern beavers, they also switch over to more of a bark diet because most of the grasses and forbs die out during the winter months. In the far north, many of the beavers never cut trees because there are no trees in the tundra areas. In Denali National Park's Grass Valley, beavers build their dams and lodges out of the scrubby dwarf willow and birch trees; beavers are also able to use the alder bushes that grow in the park for construction. They will occasionally eat alder leaves and bark, but they ignore the bush when they can get willow and birch, the beaver's main source of food.

The mass of branches and leaves in front of this beaver lodge is the winter food pile. Before the pond freezes over, beavers, kits, and yearlings will probably have eaten all of the leaves that are above water. (Len Rue, Jr.)

Beavers are also fond of many different types of roots and tubers. In her study of beavers in New York's Harriman Mountain State Park, Hope Ryden was concerned that the colony would have to move because they had eaten most of the available food trees and laid up no winter food pile. The following spring, she found that the beavers had come through the winter in good shape by feeding on the yellow pond lily rhizomes.

In time, almost every beaver colony depletes its food supply and is forced to relocate. A few years after a colony abandons a site, the dam will rot out, and the pond will become dry enough to support new vegetation. In time the area may support a new colony of beavers.

With their dams and lodges fortified and their winter food supply gathered, beavers brave the winter. When the temperature drops to 16°F (-9°C), they no longer try to break through the ice covering their ponds. At this point, except when they need to leave the lodge to get a branch for food or to defecate, the beavers curtail most of their activities.

If a predator approaches or something else frightens the beaver, it will abandon the tree it is cutting and escape into the safety of the water. The double cut in this stump shows that the beaver was scared off twice. (Leonard Lee Rue III)

A beaver tows a freshly cut sapling to the pond. (Len Rue, Jr.)

Winter

When snow blankets the beavers' pond and lodge, the animals live in a world of almost total darkness. Very little light penetrates the snow-covered lodge. Beavers cannot see well in the dark, so during the winter they rely on their sense of touch. Beavers also rely on their memory of their surroundings. Just as a person can walk through a familiar house in the dark, the beaver is able to leave the lodge, secure food from the storage pile, and return in near-darkness without a problem. Beavers can swim under the ice for a considerable distance if necessary. There is often a layer of air under the ice, or at least pockets of air bubbles here and there, that the beaver can tap into. In an emergency, the beaver can expel its breath under the water, follow the bubble to the surface, and breathe the air back in again. Evidently, the expelled air is cleaned of some of the carbon dioxide as it travels up through the water.

When the beavers return to the lodge with food, they sit on the lower level to drip dry as they feed. After the beavers remove the bark from a branch, they push it out the tunnel or carry it out of the lodge when they go out for another branch.

As beavers become less active, their metabolism slows down, and they need less food. Beavers adjust their activity level to match the amount of food they have on hand. Beavers with a restricted winter food supply are less active than those with an ample supply.

In the winter, the temperature in a beaver's lodge lowers to about 34°F (1 °C), this is higher than the ambient air temperature outside the lodge. A heavy snow cover will provide additional insulation, raising the temperature slightly. The beaver's thick fur and its subcutaneous layer of fat keep the beaver warmer than the actual temperature inside the lodge. Beavers raise their body temperature even more by sleeping piled on top of one another.

Humans and most other creatures, when exposed to daylight for even a short period of time each day, operate on a circadian cycle—a 24-hour period. When beavers are confined to complete darkness, they often go on an extended cycle wherein each day is about 28 hours long. On an extended cycle the

Beavers will only venture out onto the snow when the temperature is above 16°F (-9°C). (Leonard Lee Rue III)

beavers sleep for longer periods at a time and thus need less food. As spring approaches and the days lengthen, the slightest exposure to daylight will reset the beaver's biological clock to the circadian cycle. It is only on this cycle that beavers know to breed in mid February.

Whenever possible, beavers will cut a hole in the ice to get out to feed upon emerging vegetation. (Leonard Lee Rue III)

Beavers, especially northern beavers, are monogamous, probably by choice but also by necessity. With the pond covered with ice, it would be almost impossible for the beaver to search for additional mates. Captive beavers, which may have the opportunity to seek more than one mate, have not been known to do so. Beavers appear to mate for life. If a mate should be killed, the surviving beaver, especially if female, usually takes another mate. There are many records, however, of adult male beavers who, after losing a mate, choose to live a solitary life. These widowed males quite often do not build lodges, but live in a bank burrow. Trappers have reported that large, old beavers that they catch in such locations are almost always males.

I have never seen beavers mate because it usually occurs under the ice. Lars Wilsson, the Swedish researcher, said of his captive beavers, "The scent of the female in heat is presumably enough to make the male sufficiently sexually stimulated and, when she goes out into the water in a particular way, he follows and mating takes place stomach to stomach, the animals swimming slowly forward." Dorothy Richard said of her captive beavers, "Mating took place in the water. The female floated on her stomach and the male clung to her side with his hands while he lay sort of crosswise on his side at her rear with his right hind foot extended high out of water. I have since witnessed dozens of matings and they were always the same."

In even the coldest of northern winters, a thaw occurs around January 19 and another around February 13. A break in the cold weather draws beavers out of their lodges, even if they have to break through the weakened ice. Beavers spend the time exploring and foraging for food. I have seen many

Even when the ice entirely covers this beaver pond, the beaver will be able to access its winter food pile via the underwater entrances to the lodge. (Leonard Lee Rue III)

Left: Beavers often girdle trees—eating the bark but leaving the tree standing. In the winter months, a layer of snow acts as a stepladder, enabling the beaver to reach bark farther up. Bottom: High water flooded beavers out of this lodge. Water covered the area where the snow has melted. (Leonard Lee Rue III)

photos of trees that had a series of beaver cuts on them, one above the other like a string of beads, that were made by beaver standing on different depths of snow. Presumably, the beaver had emerged from the lodge to nibble on such trees during warm spells.

Sometimes beavers may be pushed out of their lodges prematurely due to flooding. I remember puzzling over a large tree that I found girdled 7 feet (2.1 m) above the ground. There were no porcupines in the area, and I know that beavers can't climb, yet the tooth marks looked just like the work of beaver. I talked to the man who owned the land, and he told me that, during a winter ice break-up, the outlet to the lake had jammed, creating an ice dam that caused the entire area to flood. The beaver did not have to climb the tree for its meal; it merely ate the bark off the tree while floating on the water 7 feet (2.1 m) above the ground.

Ice and snow surround this beaver dam during the winter months. Snow that blankets the lodge insulates the beavers living inside. (Len Rue, Jr.)

Flooding forced one beaver family out of its lodge twice in one winter. The lodge was situated on Van Campen's brook in New Jersey. When the ice on the Delaware River broke up and jammed just below Poxono Island, water backed up into Van Campen's brook and flooded the lodge. What made the flood more dramatic was that the ground and lodge had been covered with snow that was melted by the rising water. You could easily see the high water mark above the beaver lodge. The beavers were forced out of their lodge and spent the night huddled in some dense brush. The water level dropped the following day and the beavers returned to their lodge.

Beavers and Man

Ernest Thompson Seton, one of the greatest naturalists of all time, estimated the number of beavers in North America in pre-Columbian times at between 60 million and 100 million. As Eurasia has one and a half times the land mass of North America with conditions suitable for beaver, it is probably safe to estimate that it had a population of at least 100 million or more animals prior to the year 1000. No one can be sure of the exact figure, but areas with sufficient water and vegetation had many beavers.

In the Middle Ages, Eurasian beavers were highly valued for castoreum, which was used in many medicines. A beaver's flesh was a desirable food, its tail was considered a delicacy, and its fur was made into clothing and hats. By the end of the 1400s, the Eurasian beaver had been hunted and trapped to near extinction.

In North America, beavers were abundant. Just as the bison was the staff of life to the Native Americans of the plains, the beaver was central to the Native Americans of the north. Beaver skins were used for clothing, the teeth were made into chisels, the meat was used for food, and the castoreum was used in medicine. Some tribes considered beavers kinfolk. The Native American impact upon beavers was minimal.

But as the beaver population dwindled in Eurasia and traders turned to North America as a new source of beaver pelts, it wasn't long before the North American beaver was also at risk. Beaver fur became the main item of trade. The Native Americans were able to trade beaver skins for the metal weapons, tools, and pots that were far superior to the stone tools they made themselves. Warfare increased between the tribes as each trapped out the beaver in their own territories and then encroached upon the land claimed by other tribes. While the French trapped beavers in Canada, the British established fur trading posts in what would become the United States. In 1763, the British drove the French out of Canada and gained control of the fur trade. By 1843, the constant demand for more fur had the trappers and mountain men exploring every part of North America. Beavers had become too

The high demand for beaver pelts led to the near extinction of beavers in Europe, Asia, and North America. In recent decades, the beaver population has rebounded. Today beavers that dam road culverts are considered nuisance animals. This culvert pipe has been fitted with a barrier to prevent the beaver from sealing it shut. (Len Rue, Jr.)

scarce to be profitable to trap. The introduction of silk to make top hats replaced the need for beaver fur just in time to save the animal from complete extinction in North America.

In modern times, beavers have been reintroduced in almost all of their original range, and they again number in the millions. The latest census in Massachusetts alone documents more than 60,000 beavers. In many areas, beavers are classified as nuisance animals because they dam up streams, flooding and killing valuable timber. To control beaver populations, people set live traps and remove beavers from areas where they are causing problems. During a designated trapping season, trappers may kill beavers and sell the pelts.

In North America, the beaver's future appears to be secure. Through better game management, wildlife agencies are able to control the number of beavers in some areas and utilize their water conservation efforts in other areas. Although some people see beavers as a nuisance, others realize that beavers can also improve the landscape in which they live. By impounding water, beavers prevent floods farther downstream, raise the underground water levels, and provide a home for fish, birds, and other wildlife.

Beavers are known to be quite set in their ways. This beaver insists on building a lodge next to a major road. (Leonard Lee Rue III)

Beavers have made a partial comeback in Eurasia, but the animals still face difficulties. In most areas, the beaver's habitat has been destroyed. To accommodate a growing human population, people have cut down forests and drained wetlands for farming. Industry also threatens the beaver. In the past, many beavers have died in Germany's Elbe River Basin due to water pollution.

A beaver dam caused this road to flood. Conservationists repeatedly remove beavers from areas where they cause extensive damage. But many times a new family of beavers will discover such an area and take up residence. (Leonard Lee Rue III)

Watching Beavers

Since the beavers' amazing comeback, they can be found in almost all parts of the United States and Canada that have streams, rivers, ponds, and lakes close to suitable vegetation. In fact, I think it would be safe to say that there is no section of the continent today that is capable of supporting beavers that doesn't already have them. Although my home state of New Jersey has more people per square mile than any other state, I know of four active colonies within five miles of my home.

At times, beavers may be quite secretive about where they live. Many Eurasian beavers, for example, do not build dams or lodges. This is a safety measure. But beavers cannot completely hide their whereabouts. If beavers live in an area that has trees, the trees will be cut, leaving behind stumps for all to see. Unfortunately, over most of their range, beavers will not start their activity until just before dusk, a time that is suitable for watching beavers, but too dark to photograph them. Where beavers have been given complete protection, they often extend their activity by coming out earlier and remaining active longer after dawn. I've taken most of my photographs in Canada, where the nights are shorter in the summer, or in Alaska, where it really doesn't get dark at all during the night.

To watch beavers, do not sit in a conspicuous place because all of the beavers will spot you at once. Instead, find a tree to hide behind and remain completely still. I have found that, in national parks and refuges where the adult beavers are safe from hunters, beavers have become acclimated to people, and although not tame, they overcome their fear. In my experience, the fear inherent in the young makes them far more wary. In many of the colonies where I have observed beavers, the adults came to accept me. The kits, on the other hand, would swim back and forth, slapping their tiny tails as a warning. But none of the other beavers paid any attention to them.

If all of the telltale signs of beavers are present, but you still haven't seen one, you may be able to lure them into view with an offering of food. But because beavers usually have an abundance of food, this doesn't always work. Keep in mind, too, that it is illegal to bait beavers in national parks. Where permit-

Because beavers like to eat leaves and bark—foods with a low nutritional value—they are constantly foraging for food. (Len Rue, Jr.)

ted, try attracting beavers with apples, carrots, or ears of corn. There are countless places in North America where an observer may watch beavers, but I'll just mention a few. The dirt road in Baxter State Park in Maine is a good place to see beavers and moose. Colorado's Rocky Mountain National Park has dozens of beaver dams in the stream along the edge of the main tar road going up to the peak. There are

several beaver lodges along the Old Mine Road in the Delaware River National Recreation Area in New Jersey, near my home. Thirty miles above Dawson Creek in British Columbia, on the Alcan Highway, is the largest beaver lodge I've ever seen. Grass Valley in Denali National Park, Alaska, has a dozen lodges scattered along its length. Contact the game department of any state and ask about beaver colonies—they should be able to direct you to many of them.

A beaver carries a rock to its dam. (Uschi Rue)

This giant lodge is home for a beaver family. (Uschi Rue)

Index

Bibliography

Allred, Morrell. *Beaver Behavior*. Happy Camp, CA: Naturegraph Publishing, Inc., 1986.

Buyukmihci, Hope Sawyer. *Hour of the Beaver*. Chicago, New York, and
     San Francisco: Rand McNally & Co. 1971.

Chapman, Wendell and Lucie. *Beaver Pioneers*. New York: Charles Scribner's Sons, 1937.

Grzimek, Bernhard. *Animal Life Encyclopedia, Volume II*. New York: Van Nostrand Reinhold Co., 1975.

Hilfiker, Earl L. *Beavers, Water, Wildlife and History*. Interlaken, NY: Windswept Press, 1991.

Hodgdon, Harry Edward. "Social Dynamics & Behavior Within an Unexploited Beaver *(Castor Canadensis)*
Population." Amherst, MA: Doctoral Thesis, University of Massachusetts, 1978.

Knystavtas, Alcirdas. *The Natural History of the U.S.S.R.* New York: McGraw-Hill, 1987.

Lancia, Richard A., Wendell E. Dodge, and Joseph Larson. "Winter Activity Patterns of Two Radio-marked
Beaver Colonies." Journal of Wildlife Management. Vol. 63, No. 4. (1982). p. 598–606.

Lawrence, R. D. *Paddy*. New York: Lyons Press, 1977.

Martin, Horace T. *Castrologia*. Montreal, Canada: Wm. Drysdale & Co., 1892.

Mills, Enos A. *In Beaver World*. Boston and New York: Houghton Mifflin Co. 1913.

Morgan, Lewis H. *The American Beaver and His Works*. New York: Burt Franklin, 1868.

Nowak, Ronald M. *Walker's Mammals of the World, Volume II, Sixth Edition*. Baltimore, MD: Johns Hopkins
     University Press, 1999.

Richards, Dorothy and Hope Sawyer Buyukmihci. *Beaversprite*. San Francisco: Chronicle Books, 1977.

Rue, Leonard Lee III. *Furbearing Animals of North America*. New York: Crown Publishers, 1981.

Rue, Leonard Lee III. *The World of the Beaver*. Philadelphia: J. B. Lippincott Co., 1964.

Rue, Leonard Lee III and William Owen. *Meet the Beaver*. New York: G. P. Putnam & Sons, 1986.

Ryden, Hope. *Lily Pond*. New York: William Morrow & Co., Inc., 1989.

Sandoz, Mari. *The Beaver Men*. New York: Hastings House, 1964.

Seton, Ernest Thompson. *Lives of Game Animals*. Boston: Charles T. Branford Co., 1953.

Shelton, Philip Clarence. "Ecological Studies of Beaver, Wolves and Moose in Isle Royale National Park, Michigan." Doctoral thesis, Purdue University, 1966.

Stephenson, A. B. "Temperature Within a Beaver Lodge in Winter." *Journal of Mammalogy*. Vol. 50, No. 4. (1969). p. 134–136.

Strong, Paul. *Beavers: Where Waters Run*. Minocqua, WI: NorthWord Press, Inc., 1997.

Teale, Edwin Way. *North With the Spring*. New York: Dodd Mead & Co., 1951.

Warren, Edward Royal. *The Beaver*. Baltimore, MD: The Wiliams & Williams Co., 1927.

Wilsson, Lars. *My Beaver Colony*. Garden City, NY: Doubleday & Co., 1968.

Yurgenson, P.B., editor. "Studies on Mammals in Government Preserves." Translated from the Russian National Science Foundation. Washington, D.C.

About the Author and Photographer

(Uschi Rue)

Dr. Leonard Lee Rue III has such an interest in wildlife he has made it his life's work. He has written more than 1,100 magazine articles and 28 books. Through unrelenting hard work, he became the most published wildlife photographer in North America, with more than 1,800 magazine covers to his credit. Dr. Rue is happiest when he is looking at some critter through the viewfinder of his camera.

Dr. Rue saw his first beaver in 1949 on a trip to a wilderness area in Quebec, Canada. He spent the next seventeen summers guiding canoe trips into that remote area where he encountered beavers almost every day. Dr. Rue took his first photos of beavers in 1952 on the Worthington Tract in New Jersey when he helped Walter Van Campen and his two sons, Walt, Jr. and Harold, carry transplanted beavers up the mountain to the swamp above Dunfield Creek. In 1953 Joe Taylor and Leon Kitchen, who transplanted beavers for the New Jersey Department of Fish and Game, allowed Dr. Rue to keep beavers in captivity for months at a time. Since then, he has worked with beavers all over the continent. Dr. Rue has thousands of photographs, hundreds of hours of video, and three previously published books on beavers to his credit.

Dr. Rue and his wife, Uschi, own and operate Leonard Rue Video Productions, Inc., which supplies top-quality video footage covering the complete realm of wildlife and nature subjects. With his son, Len Rue, Jr., Dr. Rue also owns Leonard Rue Enterprises, a company that includes Leonard Rue Enterprises Stock Photo Agency and the L. L. Rue Catalog.

Leonard Rue Enterprises Stock Photo Agency supplies top-quality wildlife and nature photography, both color transparencies and black-and-white prints, to advertising and editorial markets worldwide.

The L. L. Rue Catalog offers a unique line of photographic equipment and accessories for the discriminating photographer and outdoor enthusiast. To receive a catalog, contact Leonard Rue Enterprises, 138 Millbrook Road, Blairstown, NJ 07825-9234, 1-800-734-2568, or rue@rue.com. For more information, visit www.rue.com.